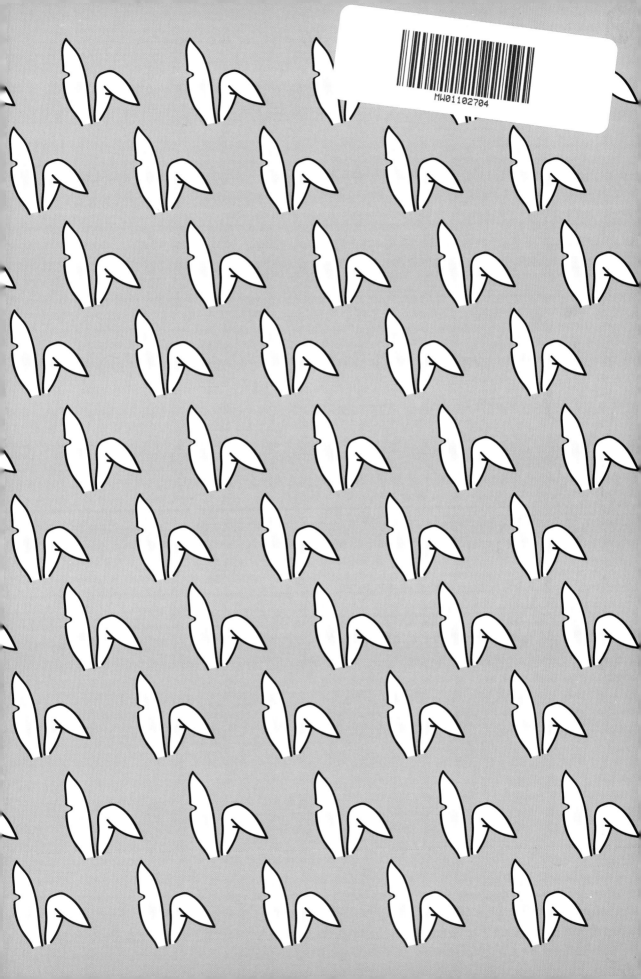

Dear Special One,

You must be very special! You would be amazed to know how many people God used to get this book into your hands. Printers, designers, computer experts, Web-site creators, pastors, business owners, housewives, children, teenagers, people on television, truckers, managers, photographers, artists, animals, friends, teachers, presidents, government officials, and parents all helped our family publish this book.

Every person who helped would like to say, "I cried too!"

This story was written about how our first daddy died. We made it through the tough times. You will too. You will feel better when you know God cares about you. Please let us know what else we can do to help you and show you how much God loves you.

In the Bible, Jesus said, "The thief comes only in order to steal and kill and destroy. I came that they may have and enjoy life, and have it in abundance (to the full, till it overflows)" (John 10:10 *Amplified*).

Abundance comes from God!

Love,

Blake Markham and Fiona Markham
Co-authors of the *I Cried Too* © book for children

The authors and creators of the trademarked I Cried Too project:
Jim & Sheila Schmidt with their children
Blake, Fiona, and baby, Sofia Joy

I Cried Too©

Written by Jim and Sheila Schmidt
With Their Children Blake and Fiona

Illustrated by Sheila Schmidt and Blake Markham

**Dedicated to the Markham Family
In Loving Memory of
Aaron B. Markham**

First Printing 2001
ISBN 0-971668-1-4

Text Copyright © 2000
Art Copyright © 2001

Golden Faith Publishing
P.O. Box 434
Broken Arrow, OK 74013
(918) 259-5000

I grew up on a special farm. I'm a bunny rabbit, you know.

My name is Abundance.

Every day I enjoyed watching the flowers, trees, and cows, but what I mostly enjoyed watching was the family who lived on the farm.

I watched one little boy do lots of fun things. Sometimes he would sneak out of his house and walk down to the pond to fish. I heard the BIG people say he started doing that when he was only three years old.

I enjoyed watching the little boy grow up. He came outside all the time. I watched him chase all the other animals. Sometimes he chased people like his brother and three sisters.

One day a little red-headed girl was walking down the road trying to run away from home. The boy ran through the woods and put on a scary face. When the little girl got near him, he jumped out and said, "Boo." She got so scared that she ran all the way to her house and never ran away from home again.

Later, when the little boy was much older and had become a big boy, he chased a big girl, caught her, and brought her to the farm. I think they got married and moved somewhere else because he wasn't at the farm much anymore.

Soon the big boy and his wife started bringing a little boy and a little girl to the farm.

The little boy and little girl looked so much like the big boy.

I enjoyed watching them play. They called the people who still lived on the farm "Meemaw" and "Granddaddy." Everyone always laughed and had a good time on the farm.

On special days there were cars and trucks everywhere. I had to be very careful of all those big tires. On one of those special days, many little boys and girls were running around with baskets, hunting for colorful eggs. It's funny, I think they thought I laid them.

Not long after that day when the grass was really green and the sun was warm on my fur, mothers everywhere were getting flowers and gifts from all their children. The big boy, who seemed so very tall now, came to the farm to see his Mom. It was the first time that his eyes met mine. I never knew we both had blue eyes.

He was always so playful. I guess it was my day to play with him because he chased me around the bushes and through the garden. He couldn't catch me, so he yelled for help. He called his Dad.

Have you ever tried to run when two big people are chasing you? I got so tired that I had to rest. So I ran into a long metal pipe to hide.

That big boy was such a good hunter. He found me. Would you believe that he and his Dad lifted that big, heavy pipe up and up and up? *Oh no*, I thought, as my bottom began to slide down the pipe. Suddenly, something very bad happened.

The pipe touched the wire high above us and the powerful lightning went into the big boy. I think he saved my life. Then I heard his Dad cry.

Soon there were voices and loud sirens. The garden was full of people. As I looked up at all the people, I saw water leaking from their eyes. I had never seen that before.

I felt water leaking from my own eyes when I heard Meemaw, the boy's Mom, say, "Even though my boy died, God loves us very much." She said, "I know my boy loved Jesus . . . I know he went to Heaven."

Then she told everyone that Jesus loved them and would save them too. She told them not to be mad at God.

I ran away to hide and thought, *Please don't be mad at me either.*

For many days I couldn't move very fast. I wanted the people to know that I cried too.

The leaves fell from all the trees, the garden turned brown, and then, everything became green again before I saw the family next.

It seemed like a long time.

The big boy's wife, their little boy and girl, and Meemaw and Granddaddy all came to the garden.

Oh no, I thought, *they'll see me. Everyone knows I'm the only bunny rabbit with a notch on my ear. I know they haven't forgotten what I did.*

Meemaw saw me first and said, "Look, there's the little rabbit . . . poor little thing. He looks like he's sad too." Everyone looked at me. I saw them smile. That's when I knew they didn't blame me.

They weren't mad at me.

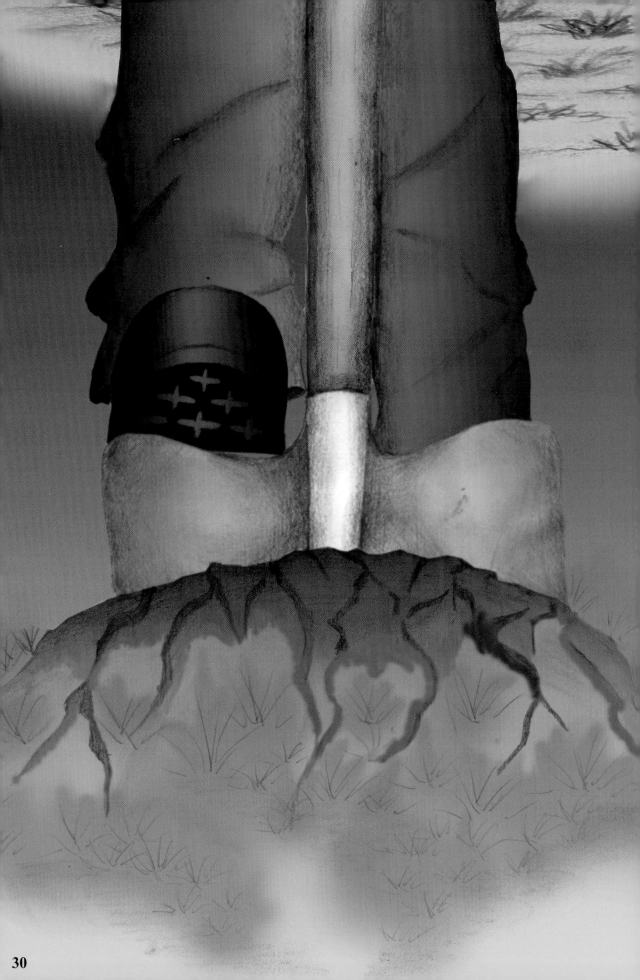

Suddenly, just like on those special days, everyone came back to the farm. There were cars and trucks everywhere. *Got to watch out for those tires,* I thought.

All the people came back to the garden. Then I saw the people do something I will never forget.

The men took turns digging a hole in the dirt with a shovel.

The blue sky turned pink when they planted a tree full of beautiful flowers.

I heard someone say that the big boy sure loved animals, but this was his favorite kind of tree.

I guess, because the big boy was gone, they planted the pretty tree so they could remember him.

Then all the people held hands, looked up to the sky, and prayed.

At that moment, I knew that they weren't mad at God either.

I felt happy again.